I0825948

# Koan Kreativity

"What keeps life fascinating is the constant creativity of the soul."

- Deepak Chopra

# Koan Kreativity

*Using Ancient Wisdom to Inspire Modern Creativity*

**Tim Ljunggren**

GENTLE THUG PUBLISHING

ISBN-13: 978-0692837580 (Gentle Thug Publishing)

ISBN-10: 0692837582



Gentle Thug Publishing

www.koankreativity.com

PRINTED IN THE UNITED STATES OF AMERICA

*To my wife and soulmate, Linda—who uncluttered my mind and my life, and who taught me what true love really is.*

*To my children—Simon, Skye, Shea, and Sarah—who are works of art themselves.*

*To my sisters—Gwen and Yvonne—who came into my life late, but who have always been there forever.*

*To my new family—Autumn, Chad, Karson, and Xander; Amber, John, Nina, Elizabeth, and Seraphina—who taught me that you can be young at any age.*

*To my adopted sisters and creative comrades-in-arms—Anne, Marnie, and Sydne—onward and upward!*

*To my first "creativity cluster"—Barb, Brad, Dawn, Dilynn, John, Jon, Mary Ann, Patti, and Tina; and my co-facilitator, Jeff—what a time it was!*

"The 'Muse' is not an artistic mystery, but a mathematical equation. The gift are those ideas you think of as you drift to sleep. The giver is that one you think of when you first awake."

- Roman Payne

# Introduction

## koan

**noun | ko·an | \ˈkō-ˌän**

Definition of KOAN: a paradox to be meditated upon that is used to train Zen Buddhist monks to abandon ultimate dependence on reason and to force them into gaining sudden intuitive enlightenment

- Merriam-Webster Dictionary

Presented as either a riddle or tale, the koan is instrumental to the Zen student's path to enlightenment; by opening and freeing the mind from both outer and inner restrictions, the "empty mind" of the Zen student is more open to insight and realization that could be achieved in no other way.

As artists, we, too, need the benefit of an "empty mind." Our own creative insights and realizations become more tangible and workable when we clear away the clutter of fear, negativity, apathy, and all other potentially destructive restrictions that we may have learned in our lives.

*Koan Kreativity* is a book that seeks to combine the ancient teachings of Zen masters with other creative insights to aid us in our artistic and creative endeavors.

# Table of Contents

"The professor leaned forward. 'But there's nothing more profound than creating something out of nothing.' Her lovely face turned fierce. 'Think about it Cath. That's what makes a god—or a mother. There's nothing more intoxicating than creating something from nothing. Creating something from yourself.'"

- Rainbow Rowell, *Fangirl*

"The whole culture is telling you to hurry, while the art tells you to take your time. Always listen to the art."

- Junot Diaz

# Koan Kreativity

*Using Ancient Wisdom to Inspire*

*Modern Creativity*

# A Cup of Tea

*Nan-in, a Japanese master during the Meiji era (1868-1912), received a university professor who came to inquire about Zen.*

*Nan-in served tea. He poured his visitor's cup full, and then kept on pouring.*

*The professor watched the overflow until he no longer could restrain himself. "It is overfull. No more will go in!"*

*"Like this cup," Nan-in said, "you are full of your own opinions and speculations. How can I show you Zen unless you first empty your cup?"*

***

As artists, there are times when we can become full of ourselves. We can forget that the creative process is one in which we're asked to keep ourselves empty so that we can be filled over and over again by our Muse.

We must allow ourselves to become perpetual students, not seeking mastery of certain artistic skills for mastery's sake, but emptying ourselves to the possibility of lessons yet to be learned.

For years, I thought of myself as a filmmaker, but I rarely picked up a camera. It was far more important for me to keep my cup full by cramming it with books, lectures, and videos on the techniques of filmmaking. How could I truly be a filmmaker without knowing the "rule of threes"? How could I call myself a filmmaker without viewing the entire film collection of David Lynch? And

Martin Scorsese? And Jean-Luc Godard? And Alfred Hitchcock?

I was afraid to pick up a camera. I wanted to cram my mind with all sorts of filmmaking information and techniques to avoid picking up a camera.

As any Zen master will tell us, we learn Zen by doing Zen. As any poet will tell us, we learn poetry by writing poetry. As any filmmaker will tell us, we learn to make movies by making movies. But first, we artists must let go of the illegitimate fears that flow through us.

We simply empty ourselves to do our work because the work is all that there is.

"To be an artist means never to avert one's eyes."

- Akira Kurosawa

# Everything is the Best

*When Banzan was walking through a market he overheard a conversation between a butcher and his customer.*

*"Give me the best piece of meat you have," said the customer.*

*"Everything in my shop is the best," replied the butcher. "You cannot find here any piece of meat that is not the best."*

*At these words Banzan became enlightened.*

***

Our work as artists demands our best efforts—regardless of the project or the situation or the moment.

Everything that we write, paint, cook, photograph, film, dance, sew—everything that we do—requires us to operate in the best way we can, within that particular moment in time.

Always.

No exceptions.

The present moment is all that we have. By living fully into it—with awareness and openness to the creative possibilities that constantly surround us—we are more equipped to use each moment given to us with both appreciation and focus.

In his book *$30 Film school,* Michael W. Dean plainly states: "Everything you do should kick ass, whether it's making a movie or tying your shoes."

Perfection is not the goal—none of our creative projects will be "perfect" (nor will *we* ever be). Simply living in the moment is enough.

In that way, every moment is the best.

"Creativity is more than just being different. Anybody can plan weird; that's easy. What's hard is to be as simple as Bach. Making the simple, awesomely simple, that's creativity."

- Charles Mingus

# Calling Card

*Keichu, the great Zen teacher of the Meiji era, was the head of Tofuku, a cathedral in Kyoto. One day the governor of Kyoto called upon him for the first time.*

*His attendant presented the card of the governor, which read: Kitagaki, Governor of Kyoto.*

*"I have no business with such a fellow," said Keichu to his attendant. "Tell him to get out of here."*

*The attendant carried the card back with apologies. "That was my error," said the governor, and with a pencil he scratched out the words Governor of Kyoto. "Ask your teacher again."*

*"Oh, is that Kitagaki?" exclaimed the teacher when he saw the card. "I want to see that fellow."*

***

We are who we are. Our essence isn't exalted by our degree, title, position, award, or any other fancy designation, nor is it muted by a lack of those things.

Our society is one that focuses on "celebrity"—our actors, athletes, politicians, and others are people that we put on a pedestal (and, at times, we love to kick that pedestal out from under them when they don't behave exactly the way we expect them to). We may give automatic credence to those who may have had a better education than us, have made more money than us, or have accomplished something we ourselves wish we had done.

As artists, we must be careful not to feed our vanities; at the same time, we must not allow ourselves to be trapped by self-disparagement. We serve our Muse, who has chosen us for the work given to us in this present moment (and our Muse doesn't give a damn about our recent five-star restaurant rating, or our recent *New York Times* bestseller, or our recent Oscar® nomination).

"Creativity comes from a conflict of ideas."

- Donatella Versace

# Every-Minute Zen

*Zen students are with their masters at least ten years before they presume to teach others. After all, learning all one can isn't as easy as learning how to ask a girl out or how to ride a bicycle. These are lessons that span a decade to master.*

*Nan-in was visited by Tenno, who, having passed his apprenticeship, had become a teacher. The day happened to be rainy, so Tenno wore wooden clogs and carried an umbrella. After greeting him Nan-in remarked: "I suppose you left your wooden clogs in the vestibule. I want to know if your umbrella is on the right or the left of the clogs."*

*Tenno, confused, had no instant answer. He realized that he was unable to carry his Zen every minute. He became Nan-in's pupil, and he studied six more years to accomplish his every-minute Zen.*

***

Creativity requires every-minute awareness, just as Zen does. From snatches of conversations that we overhear in a coffee shop to noticing the colors of the sunset reflected off our car's windshield, each moment brings with it the possibility of inspiration, while adding depth and meaning to our work—and our lives.

I've made it a habit to always keep my smartphone and a small notepad with me at all times. If I see something that catches my attention, I can snap a picture of it (or take a video of it). If I hear something that piques my imagination, I can write it down. What I capture on my smartphone or in my notepad can (and often does) inspire current or future creative projects.

In the words of Laurie Anderson (musician, writer, artist, and performance artist): "Art is about paying attention." In this way, our deliberate awareness becomes our every-minute Zen.

"Creativity is just connecting things. When you ask creative people how they did something, they feel a little guilty because they didn't really do it, the just saw something. It seemed obvious to them after a while."

- Steve Jobs

# Zen Dialogue

*Zen teachers train their young pupils to express themselves. Two Zen temples each had a child protégé. One child, going to obtain vegetables each morning, would meet the other on the way.*

*"Where are you going?" asked the one.*

*"I am going wherever my feet go," the other responded.*

*This reply puzzled the first child who went to his teacher for help. "Tomorrow morning," the teacher told him, "when you meet that little fellow, ask him the same question. He will give you the same answer, and then you ask him: 'Suppose you have no feet, then where are you going?' That will fix him."*

*The children met again the following morning.*

*"Where are you going?" asked the first child.*

*"I am going wherever the wind blows," answered the other.*

*This again nonplussed the youngster, who took his defeat to the teacher.*

*"Ask him where he is going if there is no wind," suggested the teacher.*

*The next day the children met a third time.*

*"Where are you going," asked the first child.*

*"I am going to the market to buy vegetables," the other replied.*

***

Creativity is dynamic and fluid.

Creativity is *never* static.

We may look for the same answers over and over again, but that's only because we're asking the wrong questions.

It's like that old adage: "You can never step into the same river twice."

Each time we begin a new creative project, we must approach it with new eyes and we must be prepared for results that are different from previous projects. To grow as artists, we must never settle for the "status quo," but allow ourselves the necessity of not knowing where we're going. We may think that we have an idea of how our next novel, painting, or film will turn out, but we must ultimately rely on them to inform us of their own true intentions.

We don't work on our art—our art works on us.

"When we engage in what we are naturally suited to do, our work takes on the quality of play and it is play that stimulates creativity."

\- Linda Naiman

# Your Light May Go Out

*A student of Tendai, a philosophical school of Buddhism, came to the Zen abode of Gasan as a pupil. When he was departing a few years later, Gasan warned him: "Studying the truth speculatively is useful as a way of collecting preaching material. But remember that unless you meditate constantly your light of truth may go out."*

***

Art is an all-or-nothing proposition.

As artists, we must totally and freely commit ourselves to the creative process by continuously dedicating ourselves to what our work entails.

Our light is perpetually lit by our creativity, and our artistic work is the evidence of our own "light of truth" that shines in the world.

Our perceptions of the world around us (and our insights into our own personal worlds) feed the flames that can enlighten us while bringing forth dynamic modes of self-expression through our creative passions.

We must constantly be on the lookout for new ideas; we must constantly seek out ways to better ourselves for our work's sake; we must constantly strive to hone our skills to bring forth our creative dreams and visions, and to ensure that our own "light of truth" (reflected in our work) never goes out.

As Jean Cocteau once said, "Art is not a pastime but a priesthood."

“You can’t wait for inspiration, you have to go after it with a club.”

- Jack London

# In Dreamland

*"Our schoolmaster used to take a nap every afternoon," related a disciple of Soyen Shaku. "We children asked him why he did it and he told us: 'I go to dreamland to meet the old sages just as Confucius did.' When Confucius slept, he would dream of ancient sages and later tell his followers about them.*

*"It was extremely hot one day so some of us took a nap. Our schoolmaster scolded us. 'We went to dreamland to meet the ancient sages the same as Confucius did,' we explained. 'What was the message from those sages?' our schoolmaster demanded. One of us replied: 'We went to dreamland and met the sages and asked them if*

*our schoolmaster came there every afternoon, but they said they had never seen any such fellow.'"*

***

In his book, *The War of Art*, Steven Pressfield relates a dream (or a vision) that he once had: "I was sitting cross-legged when an eagle came and landed on my shoulders. The eagle merged with me and took off flying, so that my head became its head and my arms its wings. It felt completely authentic. I could feel the air under my wings, as solid as water feels when you row a boat in it with an oar. It was substantial. You could push off against it. So this is how birds flew! I realized that it was impossible for a bird to fall out of the sky; all it would have to do was extend its wings; the solid air would hold it up with the same power we feel when we stick our hand out of the window of a moving car. I was pretty impressed with this movie that was playing in my head but I still had no idea what it meant. I asked the eagle, 'Hey, what am I supposed to be learning from this?' A voice answered (silently): 'You're supposed to learn that things that you think are nothing, as weightless as air, are actually powerful substantial forces, as real and as solid as earth.'"

Dreams and visions contain immense power for us as artists—as long as they're *our* dreams and visions and no one else's. They can drive us, steer us, wake us up, and—most importantly—help us to realize that we are not alone in our creative endeavors. Our Muse is *always* with us.

"Creativity is...seeing something that doesn't exist already. You need to find out how you can bring it into being and that way be a playmate with God."

- Michele Shea

# Incense Burner

*A woman of Nagasaki named Kame was one of the few makers of incense burners in Japan. Such a burner is a work of art to be used only in a tearoom or before a family shrine.*

*Kame, whose father before her had been such an artist, was fond of drinking. She also smoked and associated with men most of the time. Whenever she made a little money she gave a feast inviting artists, poets, carpenters, workers, men of many vocations and avocations. In their association she evolved her designs.*

*Kame was exceedingly slow in creating, but when her work was finished it was always a masterpiece. Her burners were treasured in homes whose womenfolk never drank, smoked, or associated freely with men.*

*The mayor of Nagasaki once requested Kame to design an incense burner for him. She delayed doing so until almost half a year had passed. At that time the mayor, who had been promoted to office in a distant city, visited her. He urged Kame to begin work on his burner.*

*At last receiving the inspiration, Kame made the incense burner. After it was completed she placed it upon a table. She looked at it long and carefully. She smoked and drank before it as if it were her own company. All day she observed it.*

*At last, picking up a hammer, Kame smashed it to bits. She saw it was not the simple creation her mind demanded.*

***

I once heard a tale about Ernest Hemingway in which he accepted a bet to write a meaningful story with the fewest words possible (the tale may be an urban legend, but the point remains). Hemingway reportedly thought for a moment, then wrote down, "Baby shoes. For sale. Never worn."

Six simple words. Story intact.

Arthur Quiller-Couch, who gave a series of lectures on the art of writing at the University of Cambridge in the early 1900s, said (while railing against "extraneous ornament"): "If you here require a practical rule of me, I will present you with this: Whenever you feel an impulse to perpetrate a piece of exceptionally fine writing, obey it—whole-heartedly—and delete it before sending your manuscript to press. Murder your darlings."

To "murder your darlings" isn't about infanticide—it's about removing our egos from our creative work.

It's about letting our work speak for itself, without having to prove how brilliant we are.

It's about starting over, if necessary.

It's about keeping things simple.

"The artist is not a different kind of person, but every person is a different kind of artist."

- Eric Gil

# The First Principle

*When one goes to Obaku temple in Kyoto he sees carved over the gate the words "The First Principle". The letters are unusually large, and those who appreciate calligraphy always admire them as a masterpiece. They were drawn by Kosen two hundred years ago.*

*When the master drew them he did so on paper, from which the workmen made the large carving in wood. As Kosen sketched the letters, a bold pupil was with him who had made several gallons of ink for the calligraphy, and who never failed to criticize his master's work.*

*"That is not good," he told Kosen after his first effort.*

*"How is this one?"*

*"Poor. Worse than before," pronounced the pupil.*

*Kosen patiently wrote one sheet after another until eighty-four First Principles had accumulated, still without the approval of the pupil.*

*Then when the young man stepped outside for a few moments, Kosen thought: "Now this is my chance to escape his keen eye," and he wrote hurriedly, with a mind free from distraction: "The First Principle."*

*"A masterpiece," pronounced the pupil.*

***

As artists, we may be unnerved by criticism. Others may not understand what we're trying to accomplish with our work. Our voices of negativity and doubt can wreak havoc in our artistic lives by damning our efforts before we even begin thus belittling our ambitions.

*The First Principle*—a koan about freeing our minds from distraction—is invaluable to read and understand. In it, we find Kosen wrestling with a "bold pupil" (who may or may not be an actual person). Regardless of the outer or inner criticism that Kosen experienced, he found a way to complete his work.

Like Kosen, we're tasked with completing our own masterpieces. It may take us 85 times (or more) to get it "right," but each experience draws us into the next by enhancing our dexterity, understanding, and steadfastness.

Even more importantly, we're tasked with dealing with the criticisms that inevitably accompany our creative undertakings. Our ability to maintain "a mind free from distraction" is the key to our own artistic commitment and survival, and to maintain a reliance on ourselves as worthy and gifted inheritors of whatever our Muse may bequest us.

"All true artists, whether they know it or not, create from a place of no-mind, from inner stillness."

- Eckhart Tolle

# Three Days More

*Suiwo, the disciple of Hakuin, was a good teacher. During one summer seclusion period, a pupil came to him from a southern island of Japan.*

*Suiwo gave him the problem: "Hear the sound of one hand."*

*The pupil remained three years but could not pass this test. One night he came in tears to Suiwo. "I must return south in shame and embarrassment," he said, "for I cannot solve my problem."*

*"Wait one week more and meditate constantly," advised Suiwo. Still no enlightenment came to*

*the pupil. "Try for another week," said Suiwo. The pupil obeyed, but in vain.*

*"Still another week." Yet this was of no avail. In despair the student begged to be released, but Suiwo requested another meditation of five days. They were without result. Then he said: "Meditate for three days longer, then if you fail to attain enlightenment, you had better kill yourself."*

*On the second day the pupil was enlightened.*

***

How much time do we have left in this life? Three more decades? Three more years? Three more days? Three more minutes? More? Less?

In the movie *Fight Club,* Tyler Durden drags Raymond K. Hessel, a convenience store clerk, into a back alley and puts a pistol to Raymond's head as part of a "human sacrifice" homework assignment. While rifling through Raymond's wallet, Tyler finds an expired community college I.D. card.; after repeated questioning, Tyler learns that Raymond wanted to become a veterinarian, but left school because there was too much work involved.

"Would you rather be dead?", Tyler asks the terrified clerk, "Would you rather die here, on your knees, in the back of a convenience store?"

Tyler then holsters his pistol and tells Raymond, "I'm going to check in on you. I know where you live. If you're not on your way to becoming a veterinarian in six weeks, you will be dead."

Raymond gets up off his knees and runs away, enlightened.

What will it take for us to become enlightened and finally do our creative work? How much time do *we* have left?

"The music that really turns me on is either running toward God or away from God. Both recognize the pivot, that God is at the center of the jaunt."

- Bono

# What Are You Doing! What Are You Saying!

*In modern times a great deal of nonsense is talked about masters and disciples, and about the inheritance of a master's teaching by favorite pupils, entitling them to pass the truth on to their adherents. Of course Zen should be imparted in this way, from heart to heart, and in the past it was accomplished. Silence and humility reigned rather than profession and assertion. The one who received such a teaching kept the matter hidden even after twenty years. Not until another discovered, through his own need, that a real master was at hand was it learned that the teaching had been imparted, and even then the occasion arose quite naturally and the teaching made its way in its own right. Under no circumstance did the teacher even claim "I am the successor of So-and-so." Such a claim would prove quite the contrary.*

*The Zen master Mu-nan had only one successor. His name was Shoju. After Shoju had completed his study of Zen, Mu-nan called him into his room. "I am getting old," he said, "and as far as I know, Shoju, you are the only one who will carry on this teaching. Here is a book. It has been passed down from master to master for seven generations. I also have added many points according to my understanding. The book is very valuable, and I am giving it to you to represent your successorship."*

*"If the book is such an important thing, you had better keep it," Shoju replied. "I received your Zen without writing and am satisfied with it as it is."*

*"I know that," said Mu-nan. "Even so, this work has been carried from master to master for seven generations, so you may keep it as a symbol of having received the teaching. Here."*

*The two happened to be talking before a brazier. The instant Shoju felt the book in his hands he thrust it into the flaming coals. He had no lust for possessions.*

*Mu-nan, who never had been angry before, yelled: "What are you doing!"*

*Shoju shouted back: "What are you saying!"*

***

We can learn and be inspired by other artists but, ultimately, our creativity belongs to ourselves. We alone shape and design our own creative universes, and we alone are the ones who ultimately must do our own creative work.

We must find the strength and courage to become our own mentors. We must rely on—and learn from—our own creative intuition on the journey to "becoming" an artist, with the realization that the journey never ends.

As Julia Cameron points out in her book, *The Artist's Way,* "When we respond to art we are responding to its resonance in terms of our own experience. We seldom see anew in the sense of finding something unfamiliar. Instead, we see *an old* in a new light."

"Love the art in yourself, not yourself in the art."

- Constantin Stanislavski

# The Giver Should Be Thankful

*While Seisetsu was the master of Engaku in Kamakura he required larger quarters, since those in which he was teaching were overcrowded. Umezu Seibei, a merchant of Edo, decided to donate five hundred pieces of gold called ryo toward the construction of a more commodious school. This money he brought to the teacher.*

*Seisetsu said: "All right. I will take it."*

*Umezu gave Seisetsu the sack of gold, but he was dissatisfied with the attitude of the teacher. One might live a whole year on three ryo, and the merchant had not even been thanked for five hundred.*

*"In that sack are five hundred ryo," hinted Umezu.*

*"You told me that before," replied Seisetsu.*

*"Even if I am a wealthy merchant, five hundred ryo is a lot of money," said Umezu.*

*"Do you want me to thank you for it?" asked Seisetsu.*

*"You ought to," replied Uzemu.*

*Why should I?" inquired Seisetsu. "The giver should be thankful."*

***

Whenever I complete a project and show it to the world, I sometimes think that people should thank me by (at the very least) telling me how wonderful my work is and how great I am as an artist.

Whenever I think this, my arrogance, neediness, and self-doubt are showing, and I embarrass myself.

As artists, the gift that we receive is always found in the work that we do. Everything else is just irrelevant.

I once attended a short film festival. After the showing of one of the films, the director got up in front of the gathered crowd and said, "I want to thank all of you for being here tonight. You all lead busy and interesting lives, and it's a great honor for me to have you take the time out of your hectic schedules to come and watch these films. You don't have to be here, yet here you are. Again, thank you."

I wasn't dissatisfied by the director's attitude *or* words—and I learned something from them.

As artists, we must *always* be thankful for the opportunities to share our gifts with the rest of the world.

"Art is the most intense mode of individualism that the world has known."

- Oscar Wilde

# Gisho's Work

*Gisho was ordained as a nun when she was just ten years old. She received training just as the little boys did. When she reached the age of sixteen she traveled from one Zen master to another, studying with them all.*

*She remained three years with Unzan, six years with Gukei, but was unable to obtain a clear vision. At last she went to the master Inzan.*

*Inzan showed her no distinction at all on account of her sex. He scolded her like a thunderstorm. He cuffed her to awaken her inner nature.*

*Gisho remained with Inzan thirteen years, and then she found that which she was seeking!*

*In her honor, Inzan wrote a poem:*

*"This nun studied thirteen years under my guidance.*

*"In the evening she considered the deepest koans,*

*"In the morning she was wrapped in other koans.*

*"The Chinese nun Tetsuma surpassed all before her,*

*"And since Mujaku none has been so genuine as this Gisho!*

*"Yet there are many more gates for her to pass through.*

*"She should receive still more blows from my iron fist."*

*After Gisho was enlightened she went to the province of Banshu, started her own Zen temple, and taught two hundred other nuns until she passed away one year in the month of August.*

***

Our artistic experiences can take us to many places and situations. Like Gisho, we may have many more gates to pass through and we may have many more blows to receive.

Creativity can (at times) be a difficult master; the artist is tested and measured not by how many successes she or he can amass, but by the failures she or he can endure. The artist becomes conditioned to thrive, in spite of disappointments.

There will be many times when our creative projects may be scorned by others, or ignored completely. There will be many times when we ourselves doubt the true nature of our calling as artists, and we're ready to throw in the towel (or the brush, or the camera, or the pen, or the ballet slippers).

I'm reminded of a scene in the movie *Rocky Balboa,* where Rocky lectures his son about life: "Let me tell you something you already know. The world ain't all sunshine and rainbows. It's a very mean and nasty place and I don't care how tough you are it will beat you to your knees and keep you there permanently if you let it. You, me, or nobody is gonna hit as hard as life. But it ain't about how hard ya hit. It's about how hard you can get hit and keep moving forward. How much you can take and keep moving forward. That's how winning is done! Now if you know what you're worth then go out and get what you're worth. But ya gotta be willing to take the hits, and not pointing fingers saying you ain't where you wanna be because of him, or her, or anybody! Cowards do that and that ain't you! You're better than that!

"I'm always gonna love you no matter what. No matter what happens. You're my son and you're my blood. You're the best thing in my life. But until you start believing in yourself, ya ain't gonna have a life."

Want to be an artist? Be like Gisho. Or Rocky.

"God is really another artist. He invented the giraffe, the elephant and the cat. He has no real style. He just goes on trying other things."

- Pablo Picasso

# Fire Poker Zen

*Hakuin used to tell his pupils about an old woman who had a teashop, praising her understanding of Zen. The pupils refused to believe what he told them and would go to the teashop to find out for themselves.*

*Whenever the woman saw them coming she could tell at once whether they had come for tea or to look into her grasp of Zen. In the former case, she would server them graciously. In the latter, she would beckon to the pupils to come behind her screen. The instant they obeyed, she would strike them with a fire-poker.*

*Nine out of ten of them could not escape her beating.*

***

Zen resides in the tea *and* in the pupil's motivations.

Creativity resides in the work *and* in the artist's motivations.

What motivates *us* to become artists and live out our creative dreams?

Steven Pressfield, in his book, *Do the Work,* presents us with a test to find out exactly what's behind our creative motivations (check only one):

1. For the babes (or dudes)

2. The money

3. For fame

4. Because I deserve it

5. For power

6. To prove my old man (or ex-spouse, mother, teacher, coach) wrong

7. To serve my vision of how life/mankind ought to be

8. For fun or beauty

9. Because I have no choice

Pressfield says that if we check either 8 or 9, we "get to stay on the island." If we check any of the first seven we can stay on the island as well, but we must immediately check ourselves "into the Attitude Adjustment Chamber."

"Creativity is contagious. Pass it on."

- Albert Einstein

# In the Hands of Destiny

*A great Japanese warrior named Nobunaga decided to attack the enemy although he had only one-tenth the number of men the opposition commanded. He knew that he would win, but his soldiers were in doubt.*

*On the way he stopped at a Shinto shrine and told his men: "After I visit the shrine I will toss a coin. If heads comes, we will win; if tails, we will lose. Destiny holds us in her hand."*

*Nobunaga entered the shrine and offered a silent prayer. He came forth and tossed a coin. Heads appeared. His soldiers were so eager to fight that they won their battle easily.*

*"No one can change the hand of destiny," his attendant told him after the battle.*

*"Indeed not," said Nobunaga, showing a coin which had been doubled, with heads facing either way.*

***

As artists, we choose our own creative destinies.

We can choose not to believe in ourselves, and then allow ourselves to succumb to the negative forces of our own minds (or of other people). Our work will never get started or completed, and we'll think that creativity is nothing but a waste of our precious time and energy.

We become defeated.

Or—

We can choose to believe in ourselves, and then allow ourselves to write novels, make documentaries, paint acrylic landscapes, photograph people on the street, dance the tango, and/or produce an infinite possibility of creative work.

We become victorious.

As Henry Ford once said: "Whether you think you can, or whether you think you can't—you're right."

"Creativity is the quality that you bring to the activity that you are doing. It is an attitude, an inner approach—how you look at things...Whatsoever you do, if you do it joyfully, if you do it lovingly, if your act of doing is not purely economical, then it is creative."

- Osho

# Sour Miso

*The cook monk Dairyo, at Bankei's monastery, decided that he would take good care of his old teacher's health and give him only fresh miso, a paste of soy beans mixed with wheat and yeast that often ferments. Bankei, noticing that he was being served better miso than his pupils, asked: "Who is the cook today?"*

*Dairyo was sent before him. Bankei learned that according to his age and position he should eat only fresh miso. So he said to the cook: "Then you think I shouldn't eat at all." With this he entered his room and locked the door.*

*Dairyo, sitting outside the door, asked his teacher's pardon. Bankei would not answer. For seven days Dairyo sat outside and Bankei within.*

*Finally in desperation an adherent called loudly to Bankei: "You may be all right, old teacher, but this young disciple here has to eat. He cannot go without food forever!"*

*At that Bankei opened the door. He was smiling. He told Dairyo: "I insist on eating the same food as the least of my followers. When you become the teacher I do not want you to forget this."*

***

I know of a filmmaker who rented a limousine to take him to the opening of his new film.

The filmmaker's cast and crew members drove their own cars, took taxis, or walked to the opening.

The film was never shown again. The limousine was enough.

The director's cast and crew members never worked with him again.

"The highest prize we can receive for creative work is the joy of being creative. Creative effort spent for any other reason than the joy of being in that light filled space, love, god, whatever we want to call it, is lacking in integrity..."

- Marianne Williamson

# Storyteller's Zen

*Encho was a famous storyteller. His tales of love stirred the hearts of his listeners. When he narrated a story of war, it was as if the listeners themselves were on the field of battle.*

*One day Encho met Yamaoka Tesshu, a layman who had almost embraced masterhood in Zen. "I understand," said Yamaoka, "you are the best storyteller in our land and that you make people cry or laugh at will. Tell me my favorite story of the Peach Boy. When I was a little tot I used to sleep beside my mother, and she often related this legend. In the middle of the story I would fall asleep. Tell it to me just as my mother did."*

*Encho dared not attempt to do this. He requested time to study. Several months later he went to*

*Yamaoka and said: "Please give me the opportunity to tell you the story."*

*"Some other day," answered Yamaoka.*

*Encho was keenly disappointed. He studied further and tried again. Yamaoka rejected him many times. When Encho would start to talk Yamaoka would stop him, saying: "You are not yet like my mother."*

*It took Encho five years to be able to tell Yamaoka the legend as his mother had told it to him.*

*In this way, Yamaoka imparted Zen to Encho.*

***

At first glance, *Storyteller's Zen* might appear to be a koan about imitation and melding our voices with the voices of others. Encho is asked by Yamaoka to tell the story of the

*Peach Boy* exactly the way that Yamaoka's mother did when Yamaoka was a little boy.

Yet, this koan isn't about imitation; it's about being fully immersed in the Zen (and the creative) process, no matter how long it takes—while learning how to be true to ourselves.

As artists, we have the duty of "getting it right" with our creative work by being ourselves. We can't imitate others.

Encho's mistake was found in trying to imitate the voice—and essence—of Yamaoka's mother (an impossible task) rather than staying true to the story itself (and to himself). Once Encho recovered his own true voice—and essence—he was able to tell the story of the *Peach Boy* in a way in which Yamaoka appreciated.

In the words of Ralph Waldo Emerson: "Imitation is suicide."

“Evil is committed without effort, naturally, fatally; goodness is always the product of some art.”

- Charles Baudelaire

# The Stone Mind

*Hogen, a Chinese Zen teacher, lived alone in a small temple in the country. One day four traveling monks appeared and asked if they might make a fire in his yard to warm themselves.*

*While they were building the fire, Hogen heard them arguing about subjectivity and objectivity. He joined them and said: "There is a big stone. Do you consider it to be inside or outside your mind?"*

*One of the monks replied: "From the Buddhist viewpoint everything is an objectification of mind, so I would say that the stone is inside my mind."*

*"Your head must feel very heavy," observed Hogen, "if you are carrying around a stone like that in your mind."*

***

What do we keep in our minds that weigh us down? What thoughts, fears, and obsessions prevent us from doing our art?

Our ability to create relies on our ability to keep our minds focused on our project. At the same time, our minds must be open enough to acknowledge, receive, and use any inspiration or insight that's imparted to us through our Muse.

The ballet dancer Tamara Rojo once said, "An idea never comes to me suddenly; it sits inside me for a while, and then emerges. When I'm preparing for a particular character, I look for ideas about her wherever I can. When I first danced *Giselle*, I found Lars von Trier's film *Dancer in the Dark* incredibly inspiring. It was so dark, and it felt just like a modern-day version of *Giselle*—the story of a young woman taken advantage of by others. It brought the part alive for me. Now when I talk to others who are playing Giselle, they sometimes say they're worried that it feels like a parody, and not relevant to today. I tell them to watch that film and see how modern it can be."

This "focused but open" approach to creativity allows us to be both subjective and objective when it comes to our work.

"What is an artist? A provincial who finds himself somewhere between a physical reality and a metaphysical one...It's this in-between that I'm calling a province, this frontier country between the tangible world and the intangible one—which is really the realm of the artist."

- Federico Fellini

# Kasan Sweat

*Kasan was asked to officiate at the funeral of a provincial lord.*

*He had never met lords and nobles before so he was nervous. When the ceremony began, Kasan started to sweat.*

*Afterwards, when he had returned, he gathered his pupils together. Kasan confessed that he was not yet qualified to be a teacher for he lacked the sameness of bearing in the world of fame that he possessed in the secluded temple. Then Kasan resigned and became the pupil of another master. Eight years later he returned to his former pupils, enlightened.*

***

Regardless of where we find ourselves as artists, we must be comfortable in our own skin.

To paraphrase Confucius: "No matter where we go—there we are."

Whether working alone in our studios, or presenting our work in front of a group of people, our "sameness of bearing" must be intact—we are who we are, and that shouldn't change from situation to situation.

Many artists have a "public face" and a "private face" (possibly created out of fear) that are distinctly different from each other. This takes away from the work itself, and lends itself to creating a false perception of ourselves as artists and as people.

Martha Graham, the revolutionary dancer and choreographer, addressed the subject of fear when she said: "There is a vitality, a life force, an energy, a quickening that is translated through you into action, and because there is only one of you in all time, this expression is unique. And if you block it, it will never exist through any other medium and will be lost."

In other words, don't let your true and unique voice get lost because of fear. Always be yourself—and *never* let them see you sweat.

"You can't use up creativity. The more you use, the more you have."

- Maya Angelou

# Zen in a Beggar's Life

*Tosui was a well-known Zen teacher of his time. He had lived in several temples and taught in various provinces.*

*The last temple he visited accumulated so many adherents that Tosui told them he was going to quit the lecture business entirely. He advised them to disperse and to go wherever they desired. After that no one could find any trace of him.*

*Three years later one of his disciples discovered him living with some beggars under a bridge in Kyoto. He at one implored Tosui to teach him.*

*"If you can do as I do for even a couple of days, I might," Tosui replied.*

*So the former disciple dressed as a beggar and spent a day with Tosui. The following day one of the beggars died. Tosui and his pupil carried the body off at midnight and buried it on a mountainside. After that they returned to their shelter under the bridge.*

*Tosui slept soundly the remainder of the night, but the disciple could not sleep. When morning came Tosui said: "We do not have to beg food today. Our dead friend has left some over there." But the disciple was unable to eat a single bite of it.*

*"I have said you could not do as I," concluded Tosui. "Get out of here and do not bother me again."*

***

As artists, we must learn how to let go and move forward.

We must let go of our past creative projects, whether we deem them as "successes," "failures," or something in between.

Yet, at the same time, we must recognize, honor, keep, and use the invaluable lessons that they've left behind for us.

Those lessons can keep us going for one more day—or even more.

Scott Adams, the creator of the *Dilbert* comic strip, wrote, "Creativity is allowing yourself to make mistakes. Art is knowing which ones to keep."

"One of my early mentors, poet David Wagoner, who divides the creative process into three phases—madman, poet and critic—once told me that you need to find your own magic to stay in the world of creative play."

- Sonia Gernes

# Great Waves

*In the early days of the Meiji era there lived a well-known wrestler called O-nami, (Great Waves).*

*O-nami was immensely strong and knew the art of wrestling. In his private bouts he defeated even his teacher, but in public he was so bashful that his own pupils threw him.*

*O-nami felt he should go to a Zen master for help. Hakuju, a wandering teacher, was stopping in a little temple nearby, so O-nami went to see him and told him of his trouble.*

*"Great Waves is your name," the teacher advised, "so stay in this temple tonight. Imagine that you are those billows. You are no longer a*

*wrestler who is afraid. You are those huge waves sweeping everything before them, swallowing all in their path. Do this and you will be the greatest wrestler in the land."*

*The teacher retired. O-nami sat in meditation trying to imagine himself as waves. He thought of many different things. Then gradually he turned more and more to the feeling of the waves. As the night advanced the waves became larger and larger. They swept away the flowers in their vases. Even the Buddha in the shrine was inundated. Before dawn the temple was nothing but the ebb and flow of an immense sea.*

*In the morning the teacher found O-nami meditating, a faint smile on his face. He patted the wrestler's shoulder. "Now nothing can disturb you," he said. "You are those waves. You will sweep everything before you."*

*The same day O-nami entered the wrestling contests and won. After that, no one in Japan was able to defeat him.*

***

When we finally confront our fear as artists, nothing can stop us.

But what do we fear the most?

According to the author, lecturer, and spiritual instructor Marianne Williamson: "Our deepest fear is not that we are inadequate. Our deepest fear is that we are powerful beyond measure. It is our light, not our darkness that most frightens us. We ask ourselves, 'Who am I to be brilliant, gorgeous, talented, fabulous?' Actually, who are you not to be? You are a child of God. Your playing small does not serve the world. There is nothing enlightened about shrinking so that other people won't feel insecure around you. We are all meant to shine, as children do. We were born to make manifest the glory of God that is within us. It's not just in some of us; it's in everyone. And as we let our own light shine, we unconsciously give other people permission to do the same. As we are liberated from our own fear, our presence automatically liberates others."

"Life doesn't imitate art, it imitates bad television."

- Woody Allen

# Trading Dialogue for Lodging

*Provided he makes and wins an argument about Buddhism with those who live there, any wondering monk can remain in a Zen temple. If he is defeated, he has to move on.*

*In a temple in the northern part of Japan two brother monks were dwelling together. The elder one was learned, but the younger one was stupid and had but one eye.*

*A wandering monk came and asked for lodging, properly challenging them to a debate about the sublime teachings. The elder brother, tired that day from much studying, told the younger one to take his place. "Go and request the dialogue in silence," he cautioned.*

*So the young monk and the stranger went to the shrine and sat down.*

*Shortly afterwards the traveler rose and went in to the elder brother and said: "Your young brother is a wonderful fellow. He defeated me."*

*"Relate the dialogue to me," said the elder one.*

*"Well," explained the traveler, "first I held up one finger, representing Buddha, the enlightened one. So he held up two fingers, signifying Buddha and his teaching. I held up three fingers, representing Buddha, his teaching, and his followers, living the harmonious life. Then he shook his clenched fist in my face, indicating that all three come from one realization. Thus he won*

*and so I have no right to remain here." With this, the traveler left.*

*"Where is that fellow?" asked the younger one, running in to his elder brother.*

*"I understand you won the debate."*

*"Won nothing. I'm going to beat him up."*

*"Tell me the subject of the debate," asked the elder one.*

*"Why, the minute he saw me he held up one finger, insulting me by insinuating that I have only one eye. Since he was a stranger I thought I would be polite to him, so I held up two fingers, congratulating him that he has two eyes. Then the impolite wretch held up three fingers, suggesting that between us we only have three eyes. So I got mad and started to punch him, but he ran out and that ended it!"*

***

"I was an English major at the University of Minnesota, and I was very shy, which many people misinterpreted as intelligence," Garrison Keillor once said. "On the basis of that wrong impression, I became the editor of the campus literary magazine."

As artists, we (or our creative work) may be interpreted by others in ways that we never intended.

We all react to art—and to life, for that matter—through the experiences that we've already lived through and the opinions we've already formed. Those experiences and opinions are vastly different and create a unique perspective.

However, once we complete a project and put it out into the world, we give the world permission to do with it as it pleases. We can certainly tell the world what's behind our creative process and work. Yet, in the end, it's still up to the world to experience and interact with our art in its own subjective way.

"A truly creative person rids him or herself of all self-imposed limitations."

- Gerald G. Jampolsky

# The Most Valuable Thing in the World

*Sozan, a Chinese Zen master, was asked by a student: "What is the most valuable thing in the world?"*

*The master replied: "The head of a dead cat."*

*"Why is the head of a dead cat the most valuable thing in the world?" inquired the student.*

*Sozan replied: "Because no one can name its price."*

***

What's the most valuable thing for you as an artist? What's its price?

If you answered, "The most valuable thing for me as an artist is the ability to continue doing my work with an open heart and an empty mind," then you've already discovered the most priceless thing in the world.

We live in a society that attempts to place a dollar amount on everything that we do—including our creativity.

How many books did we sell? What was our weekend take at the box office? How many venues did we cash in on with our new rock band? How's our designer fashion line holding up financially?

While it's certainly nice to get paid for our creative work, we do the work because we must. We have no option. Either we do the work, or it doesn't get done.

And, if our work doesn't get done, it's gone forever.

Who can put a price tag on that?

"Creativity is a type of learning process where the teacher and pupil are located in the same individual."

- Arthur Koestler

# Is That So?

*The Zen master Hakuin was praised by his neighbors as one living a pure life.*

*A beautiful Japanese girl whose parents owned a food store lived near him. Suddenly, without any warning, her parents discovered she was with child.*

*This made her parents angry. She would not confess who the man was, but after much harassment at last named Hakuin.*

*In great anger the parent went to the master. "Is that so?" was all he would say.*

*After the child was born it was brought to Hakuin. By this time he had lost his reputation, which did not trouble him, but he took very good care of the child. He obtained milk from his neighbors and everything else he needed.*

*A year later the girl-mother could stand it no longer. She told her parents the truth - the real father of the child was a young man who worked in the fishmarket.*

*The mother and father of the girl at once went to Hakuin to ask forgiveness, to apologize at length, and to get the child back.*

*Hakuin was willing. In yielding the child, all he said was: "Is that so?"*

***

What shows up on our creative doorsteps?

What does our Muse bring us that may be totally unexpected?

To be artists, we must always be open and receptive to new experiences and ideas in our lives (and not judge them as "good" or "bad") which may lead us to new possibilities and new inspiration for our creative work.

Stephen Nachmanovitch, the musician, author, computer artist, and educator, once wrote: "Creativity can replace conformity as the primary mode of social being. We can cling to that which is passing, or has already passed, or we can remain accessible to—even surrender to—the creative process, without insisting that we know in advance the ultimate outcome for us, our institutions, or our planet. To accept this challenge is to cherish freedom, to embrace life, and to find meaning."

“Sometimes you've got to let everything go—purge yourself. If you are unhappy with anything...whatever is bringing you down, get rid of it. Because you'll find that when you're free, your true creativity, your true self comes out.”

- Tina Turner

# Final Words and One Last Koan

The filmmaker (and an avid practitioner of Transcendental Meditation) David Lynch wrote a remarkable book on creativity entitled *Catch the Big Fish*; in that book, he gives advice to all artists which we should take to heart: "It's such a tricky business. You want to do your art, but you've got to live. So you've got to have a job, and then sometimes you're too tired to do your art.

"But if you love what you're doing, you're going to keep doing it anyway. I've been very lucky. Along the way, there are people who help us. I've had plenty of people in my life who've helped me to go to the next step. And you get that help because you've done something, so you have to keep doing it.

"So much of what happened to me is good fortune. But I would say: Try to get a job that gives you some time; get your sleep and a little bit of food; and work as much as you can. There's so much enjoyment in doing what you love. Maybe this will open doors, and you'll find a way to do what you love. I hope you do."

I hope you do, too.

Blessings and good fortune on your artistic adventures and endeavors!

And here's the last koan of this book:

*Question: Why can't a Zen master vacuum under the sofa?*

*Answer: Because she or he has no attachments.*

"Don't be satisfied with stories, how things have gone with others. Unfold your own myth."

- Jalahuddin Rumi

# About the Author

Tim Ljunggren is an Episcopal priest, a filmmaker, a writer, and a painter. He published and edited the flash fiction e-zine *insolent rudder* from 2001 until 2009, which was named by *Poets & Writers* magazine as one of the top literary sites on the internet. Ljunggren's own flash fiction stories have been published in numerous literary magazines. He is currently working on a documentary entitled *Big Sky Creativity: Montana Artists and Their Passions,* along with other short film projects.

Since 2001, Ljunggren has been facilitating "creativity clusters" to inspire and cajole people to reconnect with their creativity.

Ljunggren lives in Montana with his wife, Linda, and their three dogs (Benji, Cajun, and Ranger).

www.ingramcontent.com/pod-product-compliance
Lightning Source LLC
LaVergne TN
LVHW020638100826
845148LV00012B/2236

*9780692837580*